For Lily, Anaya
& Roxy xxx
—SGC

Penguin
Random
House

Author Sital Gorasia Chapman
Illustrator Susanna Rumiz

Editor Laura Gilbert
Senior Designer Elle Ward
US Senior Editor Shannon Beatty
Math Consultant Steph King
Production Editor Abi Maxwell
Production Controller Magdalena Bojko
Jacket Coordinator Magda Pszuk
Deputy Art Director Mabel Chan
Publisher Francesca Young
Publishing Director Sarah Larter

First American Edition, 2023
Published in the United States by DK Publishing
1745 Broadway, 20th Floor, New York, NY 10019

23 24 25 26 27 10 9 8 7 6 5 4 3 2 1
001–332641–May/2023

ISBN: 978-0-7440-8025-4

DK books are available at special discounts when
purchased in bulk for sales promotions, premiums, fund-
raising, or educational use. For details, contact: DK
Publishing Special Markets, 1745 Broadway, 20th Floor,
New York, NY 10019
SpecialSales@dk.com

Printed and bound in China

For the curious
www.dk.com

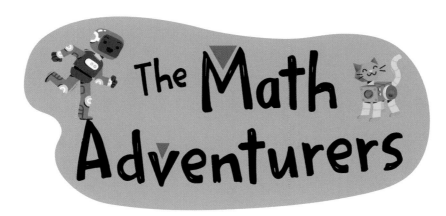

The Math Adventurers

A Day at the Zoo

Beep woke up at 7 o'clock,
excited for the day.
She's going with Boots to the zoo
to see the animals play.

You can measure time with a clock or a watch. The little hand points to the hour and the big hand points to the minute.

big hand

little hand

Lemurs in their playground.
Penguins in the pool.

Lions lounging in the sun.
Hippos keeping cool.

There are 60 seconds in a minute. One second is about as long as it takes to say "one hippopotamus". Can you count to "60 hippopotamus"?

Chimps being silly,
making the hyenas laugh.

Beep was counting down the seconds
to meet the new giraffe.

They brushed their teeth and packed a bag and left at half past eight.

After 60 minutes on the bus, they lined up at the gate.

There are 60 minutes in an hour.

"Two tickets for the zoo, please.
We'd like to feed the giraffe."

"Please meet at the treehouse
in an hour and a half.

Keep an eye on the time
and make sure you're not late.
Exactly at 11 o'clock
the zookeepers close the gate."

They stepped into a world of wonder,
with lots to see and do.
Beep and Boots had a blast
as they explored the zoo.

ELEPHANTS

At 10 o'clock they rode the mini train around the grounds.

LIONS

RHINOS

They went over, under, up, and down, and enjoyed the sights and sounds.

They saw gibbons and gorillas,
a white rhino, and her calf.
Then Boots reminded Beep
that they should get to the giraffe.

GIRAFFE
FEEDING AT
11 O'CLOCK

There are 24 hours in a
day. That's how long the
Earth takes to turn all the
way around.

GIRAFFE
FEEDING AT
11 O'CLOCK

It was half an hour to feeding time,
which happens just once a day.
"That's lots of time," said Beep,
"we're only 15 minutes away."

13

A delicious smell filled the air
and Beep stopped in her tracks.

Her tummy made a rumble
when she saw the tasty snacks.

There are five minutes
between each hour
mark on a clock.

GIRAFFE
FEEDING AT
11 O'CLOCK

Boots stared at the big hand,
another five minutes ticked past.
The line was moving super slow,
but Beep said "I'll be fast."

At last, with just a second to spare,
it was Beep's turn to choose.
Boots tapped her paws impatiently.
There was no time to lose.

It was a quarter of 11.
They could make it just in time.
As long as there were no delays
they would be just fine.

But...

As they turned the corner
the path ahead was blocked.

Sundials were the first known clocks. They use the position of the shadow cast by the sun as it moves through the day to measure time. Too bad they don't work at night!

They'd have to go the long way around before the gate was locked.

Beep turned on her turbo boots
and soon the two were speeding,

all the way around the zoo
to the treehouse for the feeding.

They turned right by the tigers,
then turned left before the bears.

They zipped on past the zebras
and whizzed past hopping hares.

Then they shuddered and juddered
and ran out of power.
The turbo boots stopped
as the clock struck the hour.

GIRAFFES

But the giraffes were in sight—just seconds away.
Beep hurried up to the gate.
"We made it!" she cried. "We made it...

"...too late!"

Beep watched sadly through the bars
as the giraffes were fed their lunch—
healthy leaves and branches.
Munch. Munch. Munch.

"I'm sorry, Boots. Let's go home."
She slowly shuffled away.
But someone caught hold of her bag
and wanted her to stay.

The littlest giraffe didn't want to be fed.
He didn't want greens to eat.

He wanted their crunchy popcorn—
a much tastier treat!

GLOSSARY

Measuring Time
Here are some words that we use for the passing of time.

Calendar—a chart to show the days, weeks, and months in a year

Second—a unit of time. There are 60 seconds in one minute

Minute—a unit of time. There are 60 minutes in one hour

Hour—a unit of time. There are 24 hours in one day

Day—a unit of time. There are 7 days in one week

Week—a unit of time. There are 52 weeks in one year

Month—a unit of time. There are 12 months in one year

Year—the time it takes the Earth to orbit the sun. There are 365 days in a year (or 366 days in a leap year)

Quarter of—45 minutes past the hour—big hand points to 9

Quarter past—15 minutes past the hour—big hand points to 3

O'clock—an o'clock time is when the big hand points to 12 and the small hand points to the hour

Half past—30 minutes past the hour—big hand points to 6

Describing Time

Here are some words that we use to describe and compare time.

Morning—the early part of the day; when the sun begins to rise until 12 o'clock noon

Afternoon—the part of the day from 12 o'clock noon until the sun begins to set

Evening—the later part of the day; from the end of the afternoon until bedtime

Today—the present day

Tomorrow—the day after today

Yesterday—the day before today

Quicker—when something takes a shorter time

Slower—when something takes a longer time

Earlier—when something happened before

Later—when something happens after

QUESTIONS

1. What time is it?

2. How many minutes are there in 1½ hours?

3. Lions sleep for at least 16 hours a day. For how many hours are they awake?

4. Beep and Boots rode the mini train at 10 o'clock in the morning. How many hours until noon?

5. If it takes 15 minutes to walk to the park and you leave at 2 o'clock, what time will you arrive?

6. How many hours are there in a whole day?

7. Which is later— morning or evening?

8. What time is it?

9. How many days are there until your birthday?

10. How many times can you count to 10 in one minute?

Answers: see p.32

ANSWERS

1. 3 o'clock
2. 90 minutes
3. 8 hours
4. 2 hours

5. 2:15
6. 24 hours
7. Evening
8. 9:15